1 MONTH OF
FREE
READING

at

www.ForgottenBooks.com

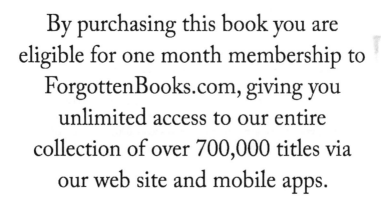

By purchasing this book you are eligible for one month membership to ForgottenBooks.com, giving you unlimited access to our entire collection of over 700,000 titles via our web site and mobile apps.

To claim your free month visit:

www.forgottenbooks.com/free616535

ISBN 978-0-483-85651-6
PIBN 10616535

This book is a reproduction of an important historical work. Forgotten Books uses
state-of-the-art technology to digitally reconstruct the work, preserving the original format
whilst repairing imperfections present in the aged copy. In rare cases, an imperfection in
the original, such as a blemish or missing page, may be replicated in our edition. We do,
however, repair the vast majority of imperfections successfully; any imperfections that
remain are intentionally left to preserve the state of such historical works.

THE SALIENT
AND OTHER POEMS

By
T. A. GIRLING

T. A. Girling 9.8.18

LONDON :
CECIL PALMER & HAYWARD
OAKLEY HOUSE, BLOOMSBURY ST.

FIRST
EDITION
1 9 1 8
COPY-
RIGHT

PREFACE

THESE poems, with one exception, were written by me, an officer with the Canadian Forces, in the forward area, and I am encouraged to put them into book form, not on account of any literary merit, but because of a demand for copies, so great that it is beyond my power to supply them, from those who, being at the Front, appreciate the effort I have made to picture things as they really are.

T. A. GIRLING.

CONTENTS

MOUNT SIR DONALD

THOU rear'st thy head, Sir Donald,
　　Above the Glacier white,
Above the mighty ranges
　　Of fair Columbia's height :
Thy rugged form, Sir Donald,
　　Thy naked crest on high,
In giant mould and feature bold
　　Defiant dim the sky.

No friendly woods, Sir Donald,
　　Shelter thy lonely height ;
The rain, the cold, the tempest,
　　Thou bear'st in unclothed might.
Low on thy sides, Sir Donald,
　　The humbled clouds drift by,
And on thy breast, a virgin guest,
　　The pure white snow doth lie.

The rising sun, Sir Donald,
　　With glory gilds thy crest,
And purple skies enshroud thee
　　At evening's hour of rest.
The coy pale moon, Sir Donald,
　　Hides shyly at thy side,
'Mid stars that light, like beacons bright,
　　Steadfast thou dost abide.

9

Thy head bows not, Sir Donald,
    Beneath the load of time :
No changes spoil thy greatness.
    No shadows dim thy prime.
High o'er the world, Sir Donald,
    Thou dwell'st in realms unknown,
Rocky and bare, serene and fair,
    Majestic, great, alone.

DUMB HEROES

THERE's a D.S.O. for the Colonel,
  A Military Cross for the Sub,
A Medal or two when we all get through,
  And a bottle of wine with our grub.

There's a stripe of gold for the wounded,
  A rest by the bright sea-shore,
And a service is read when we bury our
    dead,
  Then our country has one hero more.

But what of our poor dumb heroes,
  That are sent without choice to the
    fight,
That strain at the load on the shell-swept
    road
  As they take up the rations at night?

They are shelling on Hell Fire corner,
  Their shrapnel fast burst o'er the
    square,
And the bullets drum as the transports
    come
  With the food for the soldiers there.

The halt till the shelling is over,
  The rush through the line of fire,
The glaring light in the dead of night,
  And the terrible sights in the rear:

It's the daily work of the horses,
    And they answer the spur and rein,
With quickened breath 'mid the toll of
    death
    In the mud and the holes and the rain.

There's a fresh-healed wound on the
    chestnut,
    The black mare's neck has a mark,
The brown mules now mute, most keep
    the same gait,
    As the one killed last night in the dark.

But they walk with the spirit of heroes,
    They dare not for medals or cross,
But for duty alone, into perils unknowh
    They go, never counting their loss.

There's a swift, painless death for the
    hopeless,
    With a grave in a shell-hole or field,
There's a hospital base for the casualty
    case,
    And a vet. for those easily healed :

But there's never a shadow of glory,
    A cheer or a speech in their praise,
As patient and true they carry us
    through
    With the limbers on shot-riven ways.

So here's to dumb heroes of Britain
Who serve her as nobly and true
As the best of her sons, 'mid the roar of
the guns,
And the best of her boys on the blue.

They are shell-shocked, they're bruised,
and they're broken,
They are wounded and torn as they
fall,
But they're true and they're brave to
the very grave,
And they're heroes—one and all.

Written near YPRES, 1916.

MADONNA

Aloft the Virgin of the Earth,
  O'er the cathedral dome,
Upheld the Saviour of the world
  Towards the heavenly home ;
And smiling France looked up and
    blessed
  The hope of life to be,
The Virgin and the little babe,
  God's immortality.

But when the cruel hand of war
  Has wrecked her pictured shrine,
She stoops, the mother of the world,
  In pitying form divine,   .
And holds outstretched o'er bleeding
    France
  The hopes of hearts bowed down
That deeper peace and lasting love
  A bloody war may crown.

O tortured souls, take now the babe
  Within your homes to reign,
That there may grow diviner thoughts
  Through days of toil and pain.
A little babe, a newborn France
  Live purified by strife,—
The holy Virgin of the earth
  Bows down to give you life.
                    Albert, *September*, 1916.

THE TROUBLES OF A TRANSPORT OFFICER

Yes, everything's a worry
   In the life of a T.O.,
There's always so much hurry,
   So much rushing to and fro,
There's always something pressing,
   Some extra work to do,
And you never get a blessing
   Whatever you put through.
From morning until evening,
   In rain, and cold, and shine,
It is worry, hurry, scurry
   In the Transport line.

The Q.M. wants a limber,
   The Colonel wants his horse,
We've got to haul more timber,
   And the usual work of course,
Send three men to headquarters,
   Two kits to catch the train,
A team for the Trench Mortars,
   Report your strength again.
From early morn till evening,
   And even while I dine,
It's worry, hurry, scurry
   In the Transport line.

15

The horses all need shoeing,
    The grey has kicked his mate,
The harness wants renewing,
    And the men get up too late ;
The water cart is leaking,
    The Sergeant's got the *grippe*,
The G.S.'s waggons squeaking,
    There are twenty mules to clip.
There's always something needed,
    And all the trouble's mine,
It's worry, hurry, scurry
    In the Transport line.

Though the bullets whistled by me,
    And the whiz-bangs made me sweat,
In the trenches wet and slimy,   .
    Yet I wish I was there yet,
For they didn't always chase me,
    By runner, wire or 'phone,
Or come in rage to face me,
    Or speak in injured tone ;
You're everybody's batman,
    No work can you decline,
In the hurry, worry, scurry
    Of the Transport line.

When this blessed war is over,
    And I sit at home at ease,
I shall no more be a rover
    With the Transport o'er the seas.

But the weather's most depressing,
   And the whisky's getting low,
My cough gets more distressing,
   So it's time for me to go ;
Here's another message coming,—
   You can always tell the sign ,
Of the hurry, worry, scurry
   In the Transport line.

THE VIGIL

THE dawn has come, the long dark night
    is past,
  And all the gloomy shadows fly away ;
My watch is o'er, I am a knight at last,
  My soul is quickened with the breaking
    day.

Yet sweet it is awhile to linger still
  And ponder o'er the watches of the
    night,
To test the chastened impulse of my will,
  And know myself anew by morning
    light.

Proud knelt I down at closing of the day,
  My valour tested and my courage
    known,
Before the altar glorious deeds I lay,
  And claimed the guerdon for my
    strength alone.

Yet with the creeping shadows of the
    dark
  Came gloomy doubts which once my
    soul oppressed
With sometimes terror none but I could
    mark,
  And thoughts and deeds ignoble, not
    confessed.

How in the battle fame I always sought,
  Or strove in hope of ransom, gold, or
    power,
Or for the love of maiden fair I fought,
  Or to revenge some evil bygone hour.

And in the hallowed stillness of the night
  It seemed a paltry thing to strive and
    slay,
To wound and maim for pleasure of the
    fight,
  Or for the fleeting praises of a day.

What makes a knight more noble than a
    squire ?
  How better than the hirelings in his
    train ?
Is not to all the selfish same desire ?—
  They fight for power, or gold, or love,
    or fame.

Then, as dejected hung my humble head,
  Through the east window shone a
    glorious star,
A low sweet light over the altar shed
  And formed the cross with glory from
    afar.

What glory this ? O Christ, Thou didst
    atone,
  Not in bright arms as lieth by my side,

But naked, wretched, wounded and
    alone,
    To save mankind wert crucified, and
      died.

So wretched is my soul, so dead my
    pride,
    Wouldst Thou too bid me take the ·
      sword and mail ?
E'en so I take the Cross on which Thou
    died,
    And in the battle o'er Thy foes prevail.

Then in the brightness of the rising star
    I saw a glory higher than my own,
A wondrous purpose and a goal afar,
    Leading me on to courage yet un-
      known.

I kneel, Thy knight, O Lord, naked my
    breast,
    Clothed but in armour to defend Thy
      right,
My sword shall strike, my lance shall lie
    in rest
    Only to conquer o'er Thy foemen's
      might.

Thou diedst for me, my life is Thine to
    take,
    Come life, come death, I fear not while
      I fight

To conquer over darkness evils make,
  And shed more glory on Thy dying
    might.

My strength is Thine, O Christ, give me
    the power
  To conquer when I strike in manhood's
    name,
But to forego the pride of victory's hour,
  No fight for vengeance, gold, nor love,
    nor fame.

What fame may come, the glory is not
    mine,
  But knighthood sanctified and blessed
    by Thee,
What love, what gifts, so that Thy glory
    shine,
  I take and use them with humility.

The dawn has come, that glory lights my
    face,
  My body's weary but my soul is
    blessed ;
I take my armour only in Thy grace
  And fight for weal or woe Thy knight
    confessed.

THE BOND

Up from the cheerless billets,
   From trenches and listening post,
From huts, and dugouts, and gunpits,
   From the hearts of a watching host,
In the dark drear night of danger,
   When the soul can hide its pain,
Comes the striving, yearning, longing
   For the love of a home again.

Like the misty veil of morning,
   When the sun draws back the dew,
The pure, bright, quickened memories
   Turn back to home anew.
From lonely hearts of Britain
   The love that made them brave,
Returns to seek communion
   With those it left to save.

It heeds not the hungry waters,
   Nor distance, nor time can pen,
From the longing call of their dear ones,
   The love of a million men.
From husband, and father, and brother,
   Companion, and lover, and son,
The love of a nation is passing
   With the sound of the midnight gun.

In the treasured home of Britain,
In cottage, and villa, and hall,
With glistening eyes of watching,
Is an answer to the call ;
And the truth, and patience of woman,
In the pain that she bears alone,
Gives back to the heart that seeks it
The love that is all its own.

They vaunt of the power to conquer
In the massed and heated guns,
But the matchless might of Britain
Lies deep in the heart of her sons.
The hard, stern road of duty,
The unseen cloud above,
Are one in Britain's glory,
The conquering power of love.

21st January, 1917.

AN IDYLL OF THE WAR

He came into the billet,
  A captain worn with care,
For two weeks' rest from Ypres,
  Then on,—he knew not where.
He greeted her so gently
  And smiled through tired eyes,
When all that homely comfort
  He saw with glad surprise.

She met him at the doorway
  And gave him welcome true,
For she had two dear brothers
  At Verdun, fighting too.
She watched his needs and tended
  With willing cheerful face,
Her brown eyes shone with kindness,
  Her lithe form moved with grace.

He rode a gallant charger,
  Like Launcelot of old,
His nickel shone like silver,
  His brass-work gleamed like gold.
A sergeant followed after,
  A batman waited near,
He seemed so strong and forceful,
  So free from pride or fear.

And she was young and merry,
  And full of winsome ways,
Yet with a heart beneath them
  That shone with ruby rays.
Her voice was softest music,
  Her laugh was like the stream,
Her sadness a deep symphony,
  Her pensiveness a dream.

He tried to learn their language,
  And touch the thought that blends,
He told her of his country,
  His work, his home, his friends.
She spoke in broken English,
  And wondered oft and sighed,
And found in him a comrade
  In whom she might confide.

They played at draughts together,
  But lingered o'er the game
To talk of times and places,
  And thoughts they'd had the same.
The long war was forgotten
  In nature, flowers, and skies,
And poetry, and laughter ;
  They walked in Paradise.

He came into the billet
  With trouble on his brow,
The smile fled from her features,
  She was the woman now.

She came and sat beside him,
  He took her pretty hand,
And told her all his worry,—
  He knew she'd understand.

She was a gentle French girl,
  He needed help that day,
So is it any wonder
  That love should show the way ?
His worries seem to vanish,
  And just for five days' flight
She was his gentle Marie,
  He was her khaki knight.

Then out into the darkness
  He rode before the train,
And all night through his Marie
  Was at his side again.
While lonely as a widow
  She wept the whole night through,
For he was gone for ever,—
  The first love that she knew.

Ah ! was it wasted pity ?
  And was it broken troth ?
They loved without a future,
  They kissed without an oath ;
Or were it Heaven-sent blessing
  When exiled soldiers fight,
If every gentle Marie
  Might find her khaki knight ?

FAR AWAY

WITH equipment strapped to my
    shoulders,
  And my rifle close to my hand,
My head stretched out to the ridgeward,
  I wait here in No Man's land
'Mid the litter and lumber of battle
  On the shell-churned clay of France,
Where the craters and crumbling trenches
  Bear the signs of the hoped advance.

I wait while the barrage lengthens,
  While the rifles crack on the hill,
Then the bombs explode in the dugouts
  And the first-line trench grows still
'Mid the crash of the answering shrapnel,
  Lit my signal flares of the Hun
As the final waves pass over
  To the tat of the Lewis gun.

Out here in the rain and bluster,
  Thick mud on my khaki form,
I wait through the long day's battle,
  Through the night of the snow and the
    storm,
Till the fighting surges forward,
  And the No Man's land of the past
Is a place of quiet and shelter,
  And reaches its peace at last.

27

I wait till the burying party
  Shall find me here in the clay,
Shall loose the disc from my bosom
  And take my poor trinkets away,
Then dig a grave to lay me
  Away from this weary war,
And the shell-torn crest of Vimy
  Shall cradle me evermore.

And then in the roll of honour,
  Just one feeble flicker of fame
E'er I sink in the great oblivion,
  Will be written my humble name ;
And the fighting will still press Eastward
  To the victory close at hand,
But I shall be dreamlessly sleeping
  In the quiet of No Man's land.
                              April, 1917.

BLIGHTED

A DAY in May,
  Bright sunshine everywhere
And all the sweetness of returning
    spring,
Horses upon the hillside grazing near,
The tents of happy men who laugh and
    sing
For very joy of life and Nature's waken-
    ing,
Dear flowers in woods and fields and
    birds above
Carolling happy songs of spring and love,
Then suddenly a whistling, hurtling
    through the air,
A crash—death and destruction, pain and
    fear.

A moonlight night,
  Sweet, fiery stars o'erhead,
Grey, hazy shadows over wood and vale,
The still, soft air a balmy peace has shed
O'er lines of drowsy horses and tents, like
    pale
Grey peaks where rest and sleep prevail,
So all the night breathes out in passion
    deep
The tender care of Nature while they
    sleep,—

Then suddenly a hurrying whirring in the
    sky,—
A bomb shrieks down, a terrifying burst,
    and peace must die.

A buoyant soul,
    Warm, cherished by the spring,
To love for all creation in the glow
Of rapture that all Nature's beauties
    bring,
And hold a part in that from which they
    flow,
Spring air above, responding earth below;
So holy seems the season in the heart,
No thought but love and joy can find a
    part
Until on man and beast barbaric wounds
    and death
Stifle with sudden blast the spring's
    inspiring breath.

                    5th May, 1917.

THE FLOWERS OF THE WOOD

How sweet the flowers of the wood
    Compared with those we buy,
Reared in a simple hardihood,
    Yet delicate and shy.

From hiding-place of grass or fern
    They peer into the world,
Or on the banks of rippling burn
    Their petals are unfurled.

Their charm no crystal rose displays,
    No artificial grace,
Nor decoration nor arrays
    Attract you to the place.

They are not decked to catch the eye
    And please the sensual taste
Of loitering idlers passing by,
    Or those who seek in haste.

Untarnished by the casual hand,
    For them no price you pay ;
They seek you not in garnished stand,
    Nor tempt you to delay.

But if you wander in the wood
    And breathe the perfumed air
With heart and purpose pure and good,
    They're waiting for you there.

31

The daffodil will bow her head,
   Anemones will smile,
Wild roses turn with blushes red,
   And oxeyes stare awhile.

And you must humbly stoop and take
   Their offering sweet and fair,
Only for love and beauty's sake
   To keep and tend and wear.

Oh ! soil not with a wanton tone
   The wood's fair gentle pride,
How quick they wilt among their own
   If plucked and cast aside !

'Twere better buy a city rose
   To make of it your toy,
Then hope when all its beauty goes
   The price brings someone joy.

Yet if with tender care you should
   Bear these dear flowers away,
The fragrant freshness of the wood
   Will dwell with you alway.
                May, 1916.

THE QUEEN'S GARDEN

HE wandered in the Garden
  Of Marie Antoinette,
'Mid lawn and lake and fountain,
  Green woods and rivulet,
Sculpture among the foliage,
  And round the crystal pool,
Terrace and fern and flower,
  Avenue dark and cool.

The garden whispered to him
  Of France in bygone day,
When regal taste and reckless
  Extravagance held sway.
By costly care and labour,
  Nature and art combine
To fashion 'mid the foliage
  A symmetry—divine.

It needed but the phantoms
  To bring to life the scene,
The king and all his courtiers,
  The young and lovely queen,
Romance rewards the dreamer,
  There in a sheltered bower
Reposed amid its beauty
  The garden's fairest flower.

33

A single rose coquetted
  Above her hat's broad brim,
A sweet white gown discovered
  Beauty in form and limb,
There showed in all her costume
  And gems she wore with ease,
A taste to match her beauty,
  The means and power to please.

Perfect in her adorning,
  How perfect was her face,
Her violet eyes rich shaded
  By lash of gold brown lace,
Soft rounded flawless features,
  Rose tinted ivory set,
Dream princess in the garden
  Of Marie Antoinette.

He walked to where she rested
  And touched his khaki cap,
Then asked a simple question
  To bridge a dangerous gap,
For he who seeks life's fullness
  And delves its wealth untold,
Against its hard conventions
  At times must be o'er bold.

She turned with regal gesture
  Of anger and surprise,
But melted when she fathomed
  The homage in his eyes,

From cold enquiring wonder
  Through interest let slip,
She broke to simple candour,
  And sweet-toned comradeship.

She told him of the garden,
  She knew each nook and bower,
She loved its stately grandeur,
  Its wealth of tree and flower,
Yet loved with tempered ardour,
  And moderately expressed,
As one who granted favour
  In pleasing her behest.

He longed to see the garden
  By moonbeam's mystic light,
White pathways through the grasses,
  Lakes shine like silver bright,
Tall trees and noble statues
  With shadowings grotesque,
She sighed, and smiling murmured
  That it was " romanesque."

And so a short half-hour
  Was quickly whiled away,
Then in a sumptuous motor
  She smiled and passed away.
He sought no future meeting
  Nor wished to know her name,
The freedom of the garden
  To each appealed the same.

He wandered through the garden,
   More beautiful it seemed,
For always was reflected
   The face of which he dreamed.
Alone he lingered in it
   And left it with regret,
For everywhere was mirrored
   Sweet Marie Antoinette.

Yes, still she haunts her garden,
   The Queen of all its grace,
And show to seeking wand'rers
   The beauty of her face.
'Mid Sculpture, lake and flower,
   Fountains and monarchs tall,
The Queen of Beauty wanders,
   The fairest of them all.

                    May, 1917.

THE BATTLE

THEY are packed in the fresh-made
　　trenches,
　　They have swallowed their ration of
　　rum,
And they wait for the final signal,
　　For the zero hour has come.
They are there in the order of battle,
　　With ground-sheet and haversack,
Cartridges, rations and water,
　　And a shovel slung over the back.
The bayonets are fixed on the rifles,
　　The gas-masks are on the alert,
The Mills' grenades are handy,
　　So they scramble up over the dirt, and
　　it's

Over the top to victory,
　　Over the top to pain,
Over the top where the H.E.'s drop
　　And the hissing bullets rain.
Stout hearts must keep them steady
　　And quiet their nerve-racked frames,
For they're willing and eager and ready
　　With a courage that other men shames.

All the world seems flung into chaos,
　　Full of crashing and humming and glare,
Solid earth and poor mangled creatures
　　Leap suddenly high in the air.

37

There are flares of artillery signals,
  Dense smoke-clouds and pillars of
    flame,
But the long khaki line moves forward
  With a valour no terrors can tame.
There's the short death-space to cover
  Till they get to grips with the foe,
And the barrage is moving forward ;
  So over the top they go.

Over the top to battle,
  Over the top to kill,
Over the top as their comrades drop,
  But they keep advancing still.
There's death in a hundred places
  They must pass ere the goal is won,
But there's grim resolve in their faces
  For the deadly work to be done.

There's no time for thoughts of the
    future,
  But all the good in their lives
Is spent in one swift memory
  Of mother, and children, and wives.
Then on with a courage unmeasured
  To face, as they ne'er did before,
The barbarous modern inventions
  That substitute murder for war.

The pride and strength of the nation,
    Free offered at liberty's call,
True sons of the heroes that built her,
    Pass over to conquer or fall.

Over the top for freedom,
    Over the top for right,
Over the top with never a stop
    To the goal that is always in sight.
The vanguard of honour, life-giving,
    Defenders of all we hold dear,
God guard them in dying and living,
    Our bravest and best that pass here!
                11th July, **1917**.

ANTOINETTE LEGRU

Back to her ruined village home,
  Came Antoinette Legru,
With eager steps and shining eyes,
  Along the way she knew.

Over the hill and down the road,
  The well-loved valley through,
But there, a weird and mournful sight
  Broke on her wondering view.

Where red-tiled roof and gardened cot,
  Nestled 'mid hill and wode,
Where hall and spire had towered
    above,
  And trees had fringed the road,

A battered mass of broken walls,
  And cellars gaping wide,
And trees all broken, scarred and dead,
  Appeared on every side.

Upon the rise she saw the church
  Where, in her childhood's day,
Her simple piety had taught
  To go to Mass and pray.

A shapeless wreck, yet still in death
  It tried its lore to tell,
For carven stone, and sacred sign,
  Lay scattered where they fell.

And by the village cemetery
  Where lay her kin who died,
Were wooden crosses grey and white,
  A thousand side by side.

The near-by wood, with winding paths,
  Where, in her happiest hours,
With her young lover by her side,
  She gathered fruit and flowers,

Was nothing but a tangled heap
  Of wire and stumps and poles,
With trenches dug among the roots
  And ugly yawning holes.

And he for three long weary years
  A captive with the foe,
Yearning for home, hungry for bread,
  With spirit dying slow.

At last she reached her father's home,
  A heap of jumbled stones,
And cast-off kit and sandbagged cave,
  And dirt and tins and bones.

Mutely she gazed across the ground
  Where once she used to play,
The courtyard and the orchard trees
  Had vanished all away.

41

Will nothing give a welcome home
    To Antoinette Legru ?
Is there no token of the past,
    No hope to grow anew ?

Yes, there beside a broken wall,
    Among destruction dread,
A Crimson Rose of days gone by,
    Rears up its glorious head.

It speaks of roots too deeply set
    For even war to slay,
That raise again as from the dead
    The Love of yesterday.

She saw, and, kneeling, kissed the flower,
    The beauteous living sign,
'Mid desolation all around,
    Of something yet divine.

With dimming eyes and heaving breast
    She tried some prayer to say,
Then flung herself upon the ground
    And sobbed her grief away.

IN THE FIELD, 29*th August*, 1917.

THE SOLDIER'S HOME

A SECOND storey bedroom,
   Or a camp-bed in a tent,
In time of peace was satisfact'ry found,
But the thing that gives a soldier
   The best feeling of content
Is a cushy little hole beneath the ground.

A tent is quickly riddled,
   And a house is blown to bits,
Ere the occupant has time to get away
From superfluous attention
   Of the persevering Fritz,
In his usual consid'rate little way.

So to get your usual slumber
   When located near the Front,
If the shelling and the bombing give you
     qualms,
Don't consider ventilation,
   Not for driest quarters hunt,
But rest content and free from all alarms,

In a hole of proper deepness,
   With some sandbags overhead,
Or the heaviest material you can find,
And lay your army blanket
   On the damp earth for a bed,
Then scatter all your worries to the wind.

The shells may burst around you,
  The bombs drop close enough
To awake you from the pleasantest of
    dreams,
But the vital cause of worry
  Is the chunky bits of stuff,
And they haven't learnt to burrow yet,
    it seems.

The quarters of a general,
  The soldier's "home, sweet home,"
When in the fighting area they are
    found,
Is a six by six compartment
  With the Mother Earth for dome,
Just a dinky little hole beneath the·
    ground.

25th October, 1917.

44

PEACE ON EARTH

THE Christmas snows have hidden
  The ruined town and fosse
With heaven-sent witness bidden
  To cover wreck and loss.
A silver moon is sailing
  'Mid stars up in the height,
Quiet and peace prevailing
  On this fair Christmas night.
This hour no sound of battle
  Troubles the tranquil air,
No fierce machine-guns rattle,
  Shell burst or rocket flare.
A truce for Christmas greetings,
  A peace for Christmas fare,
With warm and heartfelt greetings,
  Is granted to us here.
And round the dugout table,
  And in the trench before,
Each man as he is able
Utters this wish once more
To comrades tried in danger
  And tested in the fire,
Or to the newcome stranger—
  To all this one desire,
That Christmas next returning
  May find us with our own
By the dear " home-fire " burning
  For all and each alone.
Though how to heal the breaches
  We may not understand,

The peace that Christmas teaches
   May dwell in every land.
And out beyond the wire,
   And East, and North, and South,
This one sincere desire
   Is passed from every mouth.
The blessed Christmas season
   Unites in mutual hope,
With neither fear nor treason,
   All those within its scope.
Ah ! if a wish so fervent
   Can rise from such a host,
All other thoughts subservient
   To this they long for most,
E'en if no God in Heaven
   Sent peace down to the earth,
Must not the spirit leaven
   Awake it into birth ?
Though Nature's laws be broken,
   And " deeds of shame " be wrought,
Unpardoned words be spoken,
   And honour set at nought ;
Though hearts are hot with anger,
   And others dead and cold,
While vengeance stirs from languor
   The fiercest thoughts they hold,—
Yet this one planted treasure,
   Within the hearts of all,
Shall swell with mighty measure
   And conquer over all.

                        Christmas, 1917.

THE SALIENT

THEY come from Southern victories
   Another tryst to keep,
They march along the well-known road
Where often through the night they trode
   From Poperinghe to Ypres.

Down by the Gun Asylum
   And past the famed Cloth Hall,
Old ruins now, more battered still,
Chateau, cathedral, hall and mill,
   All tottering to their fall.

Out past their old entrenchments
   To post just lately won,
And in the night they take their stand,
In concrete fort and shell-hole land,
   Against the cowering Hun.

They march not on as strangers,
   But those who bear the brief
To shed fresh glory on their sign,
Borne bravely in the fighting-line,
   Canada's maple leaf.

The purpose of their coming
   The graves of those shall speak
Who bore the first dread gas attack
And hurled the pressing foeman back
   Or died at Zillebeke.

In Ypres' famous salient
   They claim the right to share,
Whose most heroic deeds were done,
Most hardly wrested triumphs won,
   Most losses suffered here.

And on the ridges forward
   Canadian signals fly,
And in the lower land between,
Advancing through the fiery screen,
   Canadian heroes die.

Yet forward, dauntless pressing,
   The final goal assail,
And claim for Britain's Western sons
One more great victory 'mid the guns—
   The heights of Passchendaele.

THE HORSE ALLOTTED TO X
COMPANY

Oh! I am the Company's geegee,
    The horse that belongs to the bunch,
The " Saddle him quick and lend me
      your stick,
    For I must get to Bruce for lunch."
They wobble and bump in the saddle,
    They trot me o'er cobbles and flint ;
I'm theirs for a day, as we're off and
      away
    To the places of bubbles and glint.

Oh ! I'm the mechanical transport,
    The thing that you race and you pound,
The way to get there, with a gallop and
      cheer
    When the turn for the joy-ride comes
      round ;
The slave left in bonds at the shed-post,
    Till the longest of beanoes must end ;
Then they jump on my back, and they
      cheer the way back
    By a spirited race with a friend.

Oh ! I am the syndicate *cheval*,
    The creature that nobody owns,
A sub.'s for a day when a captain's away,
    And the next day a series of loans.

49

I'm the pride of no horse-loving master,
  The hero of no mess-room talk,
And if I go lame, why it's just a damned
    shame,
  For the Company jockeys must walk.

Oh ! I'm the disgrace of the transport,
  The horse that's a constant menace ;
The shoeing-smith swears, and the T.O.
    declares
  That I'll have to be sent to the base.
My feet are a hotbed of bruises,
  My tendons are bulging with sprains,
My coat's always dry, my digestion's
    awry,—
  Just my " Company " heart still
    remains.

MOUNT ST. ELOI

Twin towers crowned Mount St. Eloi,
  Majestic side by side,
A landmark from the distance,
  A monument of pride.
They gleamed through mist and shadow,
  They caught the dying light,
And capped the hill with glory,
  Twin towers of dazzling white.

Twin towers in all things equal
  Stood forth, till they in war
The fury of bombardment
  With equal grandeur bore,
As shrapnel hailed against them
  And high explosives made
The very hill to tremble,
  Wherein their strength was stayed.

Then side by side their splendour
  Stooped to the bolts of hell,
As coping stone and pillar
  Toppled and crashing fell.
Yet month by month, sore smitten,
  They crowned the battered slope,
And flashed from suns of evening
  Their signals white of hope.

Now that the foe is driven
  Far from St. Eloi's hill,

They stand against the skyline
  Broken but splendid still.
Though equal chance they breasted
  And stood as twins before,
Yet war has laid the burden
  On one to suffer more.

          19th February, 1918.

THE WHITEFRIARS PRESS, LTD., LONDON AND TONBRIDGE.

CECIL PALMER AND HAYWARD

GUNS AND GUITARS.

By W. R. TITTERTON.

Author of " Me as a Model," " Afternoon Tea Philosophy," etc.

Cr. 8vo.   2s. 6d.   net.

A new volume of verse by this well-known author. Some of the poems contained in this volume have been set to music.

AUSTRALIA AT WAR.

By LIEUT. WILL DYSON, Official Artist to the Australian Imperial Forces at the Front.

With a lengthy Introduction by G. K. CHESTERTON. Dedication Poem by LIEUT. WILL DYSON : " TO THE MEN OF THE A.I.F."

Cloth, 6s. net.   Ready shortly.

THE HISTORY OF THE HUN.

By ARTHUR MORELAND, Author of " Humours of History."

Paper, 1s. 6d. *net.   Cloth*, 2s. 6d. *net.*

A series of clever drawings, with legends beneath each, in which the author-artist gives a humorous account of the enemy throughout the ages to the present day.   His satire is all the more potent through being restrained.

SONGS OF THE SPECIALS.

By E. W. FORDHAM.

Boards. 1s. 6d. net.

A Book for " Specials " by a " Special."   With an Introduction by G. K. CHESTERTON, and Six Illustrations in Black and White by HUGH G. RIVIERE.

OAKLEY HOUSE, 14/18, BLOOMSBURY ST., W.C. 1

Lightning Source UK Ltd.
Milton Keynes UK
UKHW012331061118
331891UK00010B/966/P